The Blockchain Explained

Understanding the Technology Behind Bitcoin, Smart Contracts, and Decentralized Finance

By Joe Correa

Published by Live Stronger Faster

This book is for educational and informational purposes only. The author and publisher are not engaged in rendering legal, financial, or other professional advice. Readers should consult a qualified professional before making any financial decisions.

First Edition

Table of Contents

Introduction

Before we can truly understand cryptocurrency, we must first understand the powerful technology that makes it all possible: **blockchain**. This term gets thrown around frequently, often surrounded by hype, mystery, or buzzwords—but at its core, blockchain is a revolutionary structure that is transforming how we exchange value, verify information, and build trust without middlemen. Whether you're investing in Bitcoin, exploring smart contracts, or diving into the world of decentralized finance (DeFi), everything ties back to this foundational innovation.

Blockchain is not just a technical term—it's a new **paradigm of digital interaction**. Much like how the internet changed communication and commerce, blockchain is changing how we **store, secure, and transfer assets**. But what is it really? How does it work? And more importantly, why does it matter to you as an investor, entrepreneur, or curious learner? That's exactly what we'll break down in this book.

In this third installment of the Crypto Wealth Academy series, we will demystify blockchain technology in clear, easy-to-understand language. We'll strip away the complexity and reveal the elegant logic that underpins this system—starting with how **blocks, hashes, nodes, and**

consensus mechanisms work. You'll learn how blockchain provides **security through decentralization**, **immutability**, and **transparency**—and why these traits are so valuable in the digital economy.

Next, we'll dive into how blockchain powers the Bitcoin network, then move on to **smart contracts**—automated, self-executing agreements that are changing industries from real estate to insurance. We'll explore **Ethereum**, the world's most popular smart contract platform, and why it laid the foundation for **DeFi**, NFTs, and a new wave of decentralized applications. If Bitcoin was the first chapter, Ethereum and its smart contract ecosystem is the next leap.

You'll also gain insight into how **decentralized finance (DeFi)** uses blockchain to eliminate the need for traditional banks and financial intermediaries. We'll walk through examples of lending, borrowing, earning interest, and trading in this ecosystem—and the risks involved. Understanding the **blockchain rails** these systems run on is essential if you plan to invest in, build on, or simply survive and thrive in the coming Web3 economy.

By the end of this book, you won't just understand what blockchain is—you'll understand **why it's the backbone of the next digital revolution**. You'll see how it connects to real-world use cases and financial opportunities, and how this once-niche technology is becoming a central pillar of global infrastructure.

Whether you're a crypto beginner seeking clarity or an aspiring investor or builder who wants to grasp the "why" behind the buzz, this book is your gateway into the fascinating world of blockchain. Welcome to the engine room of the cryptocurrency movement. Let's begin.

Chapter 1: What Is Blockchain and Why It Matters

Blockchain is often referred to as the backbone of cryptocurrency, but its significance goes far beyond digital money. At its core, blockchain is a **distributed, immutable ledger**—a shared database that records transactions and is maintained by a network of computers, or **nodes**, without needing a central authority. Understanding this simple yet powerful concept is key to grasping how Bitcoin works, how smart contracts function, and how decentralized finance is disrupting traditional banking.

The traditional financial system relies heavily on **intermediaries**—banks, brokers, clearinghouses—to maintain trust and record-keeping. Every time money changes hands, multiple institutions are involved in verifying and settling the transaction. This process is time-consuming, expensive, and prone to errors or manipulation. Blockchain eliminates the need for these intermediaries by replacing institutional trust with **mathematical trust**. Instead of relying on humans, we now rely on **code and consensus**.

Imagine a book where every time a page is filled, it gets sealed and linked to the previous page using a cryptographic fingerprint known as a **hash**. Once sealed, that page cannot be changed without altering every page after it—an almost impossible task. That's essentially how blockchain works. Each "block" of data contains a batch of transactions, a timestamp, the hash of the previous block, and a unique hash of its own. As blocks are added in sequence, they form a **chain**—a blockchain. This structure ensures transparency, integrity, and security.

But what makes blockchain truly revolutionary is its **decentralized nature**. Instead of storing data on one central server, copies of the blockchain are distributed across thousands of nodes globally. Each node verifies new blocks using **consensus algorithms**—rules that determine whether a transaction is valid. Bitcoin, for example, uses **Proof of Work**, a system where nodes (called miners) solve complex math problems to validate transactions and add new blocks. This decentralized consensus eliminates the risk of single points of failure and makes blockchains **censorship-resistant** and nearly impossible to hack.

The implications are massive. Blockchain enables **peer-to-peer trust** on a global scale. You can send money to someone across the world without needing a bank. You can create contracts that execute themselves without needing a lawyer. You can build applications that can't be taken down by a single authority. This shift is foundational—it transforms how we handle **value, identity, ownership, and governance** in the digital world.

While blockchain was first introduced with Bitcoin in 2009, its potential applications span far beyond currency. Supply chain tracking, digital identity, voting systems, medical records, real estate, and energy grids are all being reimagined with blockchain technology. The rise of **Ethereum** and **smart contracts** took things even further by enabling programmable logic on top of blockchains, unlocking a new universe of decentralized applications (dApps).

However, blockchain is not without challenges. Scalability, energy consumption (especially in Proof of Work systems), regulatory uncertainty, and user experience are still areas being worked on. But as the technology evolves, so do the solutions—from **Proof of Stake** to **Layer 2 scaling** to **blockchain interoperability**.

In summary, blockchain is a **trust machine**. It's not just about crypto—it's about rethinking how we verify, record, and execute agreements in a world that's increasingly digital and global. If data is the new oil, blockchain is the pipeline that moves it securely and transparently.

Noah's story

Noah had always been a tech enthusiast, the kind of person who built computers in his garage and beta-tested new software before anyone else had heard of it. But when it came to cryptocurrency, he was skeptical. "Just digital money for hackers and hype-chasers," he used to say. That all changed one rainy evening in January, when a friend introduced him to the world of blockchain—not with buzzwords, but with a problem.

His friend Ava had recently launched a small art licensing business, selling original digital paintings to collectors around the world. But she was running into issues: third-party platforms were charging enormous fees, buyers in different countries were suspicious of payment delays, and her artwork was being pirated and copied without proof of ownership. Ava was frustrated—and searching for something better.

That's when Ava explained how she was testing a new model using blockchain. "I can embed my artwork's ownership certificate right into the blockchain," she said. "No one can change it, and everyone can see it. I get paid instantly. No middleman. No fraud." She showed him a simple user interface where her digital painting was linked to a transaction ID on the Ethereum network. A smart contract had automatically sent her payment once the buyer confirmed receipt. It was like magic.

Intrigued, Noah started digging. He learned that blockchain was not just about crypto—it was a **system of digital truth**. It stored records not on one server, but across thousands of computers. These records—called blocks—were sealed and connected using advanced cryptography, forming an unbreakable chain of trust. Every node in the network had a copy, and no one could cheat or tamper with it without alerting the entire system.

He likened it to a global notebook that everyone could write in, but no one could erase. This wasn't just useful for money—it was a revolution in how people could **store value, prove identity, and transfer ownership** without needing to beg permission from banks, governments, or tech giants.

Noah kept reading. He discovered how the Bitcoin blockchain used something called Proof of Work to keep the system honest. Miners solved complex puzzles, not for fun, but to earn the right to add a new block to the chain. Their reward? Bitcoin. This game theory ensured that everyone had an incentive to play fair. It blew his mind. Instead of trusting an institution, you trusted math and code.

What struck him most was the *decentralization*. No one controlled the blockchain. It was like an unstoppable, borderless record keeper. When Ava mentioned she was experimenting with decentralized finance—earning interest, swapping tokens, and lending money without a bank—Noah knew he had to go deeper.

He watched hours of tutorials, read whitepapers, and joined online communities. Each use case opened his eyes: farmers in Africa using blockchain to verify crop origins; immigrants sending money home without fees; refugees proving identity without passports. Blockchain wasn't just about speculation—it was about **inclusion, empowerment, and transparency**.

One night, as he stared at a blockchain explorer showing live Ethereum transactions, Noah had a realization. "This is like watching the future unfold, one block at a time," he whispered. In a world full of misinformation and institutional breakdowns, blockchain offered a shared reality—verifiable, transparent, and permanent.

By the end of the month, Noah had built his own Ethereum smart contract, minted his first token, and launched a small DAO (Decentralized Autonomous Organization) with other developers. What started as a curiosity became a calling.

The blockchain wasn't just a technology. It was a mindset shift. One where trust is earned, not assumed. Where ownership is verified, not declared. And where opportunity isn't granted—it's coded into the very structure of a transparent digital economy.

And Noah? He never looked at money, or trust, or institutions the same way again.

Chapter 2: How Blockchain Works — Blocks, Hashes, Nodes & Consensus

To fully grasp the power of blockchain, it's essential to understand its moving parts. While the concept is simple—an immutable digital ledger maintained across many computers—the underlying technology includes several components that work together to make it secure, transparent, and decentralized. These components are: **blocks**, **hashes**, **nodes**, and **consensus mechanisms**. Each plays a key role in building trust without relying on centralized authority.

Let's begin with **blocks**. A block is a package of data that contains a list of transactions, a timestamp, the hash of the previous block, and a new hash that uniquely identifies the current block. In essence, a block is like a page in a ledger book. Once it's full or reaches a certain size or time threshold, it is sealed and added to the chain. Every subsequent block connects to the one before it, forming a chain of blocks—a *blockchain*.

The **hash** is what locks the block into place. A hash is a long string of letters and numbers created by a cryptographic algorithm—Bitcoin uses SHA-256, for example. It functions like a digital fingerprint. If you so much as change a comma in the data inside the block, the entire hash will change. This property is what makes blockchain **tamper-evident**. If someone tries to change a block, every other block that follows becomes invalid. This gives blockchain its most valuable quality: **immutability**.

Nodes are the computers that participate in maintaining and verifying the blockchain. Each node keeps a full or partial copy of the entire blockchain. When a new block is proposed, these nodes work together to validate the transactions and reach **consensus**—meaning agreement—on whether the block is legitimate. Because there's no central database or server, blockchain relies on these nodes to stay honest and synchronized across the globe.

Now comes the concept of **consensus mechanisms**. These are the rules that nodes follow to agree on the state of the blockchain. The most well-known is **Proof of Work (PoW)**, used by Bitcoin. In PoW, nodes (called miners) compete to solve a difficult mathematical puzzle. The first one to solve it gets to add the next block and earns a reward in cryptocurrency. This process is energy-intensive but secure.

Another popular mechanism is **Proof of Stake (PoS)**, where validators are chosen based on how much cryptocurrency they "stake" or lock up. Instead of using massive computing power, PoS relies on financial incentives. It's far more energy-efficient and is becoming the preferred model for newer blockchains like Ethereum 2.0, Solana, and Cardano.

Let's tie it all together. A blockchain begins when someone initiates a transaction—say, sending Bitcoin to a friend. This transaction is broadcast to the network. Nodes validate it by checking that the sender has enough balance and that the digital signatures are valid. Valid transactions are bundled into a block. Miners (in PoW) or validators (in PoS) race or are selected to add the block. Once a block is added, it becomes part of the permanent blockchain, viewable by anyone.

The beauty of this system is that no one entity controls it. Trust is distributed among thousands of nodes. If one node goes offline, others take over. If someone tries to alter the chain, they'd need to change the data on **more than 50% of the nodes simultaneously**—an almost impossible feat on a large, decentralized network. That's what makes blockchain so resistant to censorship, fraud, and corruption.

While technical, this architecture is what powers everything from Bitcoin transactions to NFT ownership to lending and borrowing in DeFi. Understanding blocks, hashes, nodes, and consensus not only deepens your knowledge of the space but also shows you why blockchain is **one of the most resilient digital structures ever created**.

Sofia, the software developer

Sofia was a software developer in her late 30s, living in Lisbon, Portugal. Her career had been spent building secure backends for banking apps and government platforms. She was sharp, methodical, and deeply skeptical of hype—especially around things like blockchain and crypto. She'd seen too many people lose money chasing trends. But when her cousin Marco, an app designer in Brazil, asked her to help build a decentralized platform, she decided to investigate—more out of curiosity than conviction.

Marco wanted to create a decentralized freelance marketplace. No banks, no platforms taking 20%, no waiting for payment. Just smart contracts. Sofia agreed to help, but only after understanding the mechanics. "Let's start at the beginning," she said. "What exactly is a blockchain?"

Marco explained what he knew. But it wasn't until Sofia started reading whitepapers, watching network animations, and playing with testnets that the pieces started to click. She discovered that a blockchain was essentially a growing chain of digital blocks—each holding data, such as transactions—locked together in a way that made tampering practically impossible.

One evening, she opened her laptop and walked through a real Bitcoin block. Inside it were hundreds of transactions, each verified, each encoded into the structure. The block had a unique cryptographic fingerprint—a **hash**—and that hash depended on the data within it. The tiniest change, like adjusting the time by a second, would completely change the hash. She was stunned. "This is like a DNA sequence for every block," she thought.

More fascinating was how each block contained the hash of the **previous** block. That's what made it a **chain**. If you changed a block, its hash would no longer match the one referenced by the next block—breaking the chain. This was the genius of immutability. No need to trust a company, a bank, or a government. The math made it tamper-proof.

She dove deeper into **nodes**—the computers that store and verify the blockchain. They weren't just passive listeners; they were active participants, constantly syncing with one another, agreeing on what was true. There was no server. No one person in charge. Just thousands of nodes reaching consensus on the truth. It was like a global democracy of data.

Sofia then explored **consensus mechanisms**. The Bitcoin network used something called **Proof of Work**—a brutal race where computers solved complex puzzles to win the right to add the next block. It was wasteful, yes, but also effective. She watched live mining activity, seeing blocks confirmed by miners around the globe. The whole system was designed so that cheating cost more than playing fair. Elegant and ruthless.

But Proof of Work wasn't the only way. Marco showed her **Proof of Stake**, where validators were chosen based on how much crypto they locked up. This meant lower energy use, faster confirmations, and still enough incentive to behave honestly. It was the system Ethereum was transitioning to—and it made her wonder if this could work at scale.

Together, Sofia and Marco built a prototype. When a freelancer completed a project, the client's crypto payment would sit in a smart contract. Once the work was approved, the funds would automatically release—no invoices, no banks, no delays. The transaction was hashed, included in a block, and confirmed by validators. Transparent. Immutable. Borderless.

Watching it all unfold—seeing data flow from user to node to blockchain—Sofia couldn't help but marvel at the architecture. It was unlike anything she'd worked on before. No single point of failure. No middleman to compromise. Just logic, code, and consensus.

In the quiet of her home office, Sofia leaned back and smiled. She no longer saw blockchain as a buzzword. She saw it as a new kind of **infrastructure**—one built not on trust in people or institutions, but on code that anyone could inspect and everyone could verify.

It wasn't just a system. It was a movement. And she was now a part of it.

Chapter 3: Smart Contracts — Code as Law

Smart contracts are one of the most groundbreaking innovations to emerge from blockchain technology. While cryptocurrencies like Bitcoin revolutionized how we store and transfer value, smart contracts revolutionized how we create **agreements** in a digital world—agreements that are trustless, automatic, and self-enforcing. They allow for the creation of applications, platforms, and systems that run exactly as programmed, without downtime, censorship, or human error.

At a basic level, a smart contract is simply **code stored and executed on a blockchain**. It runs when specific conditions are met—no middleman required. Think of it like a vending machine: you insert money, choose your item, and the machine automatically dispenses it. There's no cashier, no oversight—just logic and automation. In the same way, a smart contract can automatically transfer funds, mint tokens, or grant access when predetermined rules are satisfied.

These contracts live on **programmable blockchains**, with **Ethereum** being the pioneer and most widely used platform. Ethereum introduced a programming language called **Solidity**, which allows developers to write smart contracts that can manage everything from crowdfunding campaigns to digital identity systems to decentralized finance protocols.

Here's an example: imagine Alice wants to sell a digital art file to Bob. Instead of using a payment platform, they use a smart contract. Alice uploads the artwork and sets the price. Bob sends the money to the smart contract. Once payment is confirmed, the contract releases the file to Bob and the funds to Alice. Neither party can scam the other. The code governs the transaction, not a company or third party.

The benefits of smart contracts are numerous:

- **Trustless**: You don't have to trust the other person—only the code.
- **Automation**: Everything happens instantly and automatically.
- **Transparency**: Anyone can view the code and see exactly what it will do.
- **Security**: Once deployed, contracts are tamper-proof.
- **Efficiency**: Eliminates paperwork, delays, and manual oversight.

But smart contracts also come with **risks and challenges**. The biggest issue is **bugs in the code**. Because blockchain is immutable, once a smart contract is deployed, you usually can't change it. If there's a flaw, it could be exploited by hackers—as seen in the infamous 2016 DAO hack where over $50 million was stolen from a flawed contract. This led to a major debate and even a **hard fork** of the Ethereum blockchain.

Another concern is **legal enforceability**. While the code may execute an action, it might not have legal standing in traditional courts. There's also the issue of **gas fees**—on Ethereum, users must pay fees to run code, and during times of high network congestion, those fees can be very high.

Despite these issues, the smart contract ecosystem is growing rapidly. **DeFi protocols** like Uniswap, Aave, and Compound use smart contracts to facilitate billions of dollars in transactions without traditional banks. **DAOs** (Decentralized Autonomous Organizations) are groups governed entirely by smart contracts. Even NFTs—non-fungible tokens—are minted and transferred using smart contract logic.

The future may bring **smart legal contracts**, where real-world legal documents are written in human and machine-readable code. These could dramatically change industries like law, real estate, and insurance. Already, some governments and major enterprises are experimenting with smart contracts for **supply chain tracking**, **land registries**, and **automated compliance**.

In conclusion, smart contracts mark the shift from traditional contracts written on paper to digital logic written in code. They're not just agreements—they're **digital rulesets** that execute themselves. As you explore crypto, DeFi, or Web3, understanding smart contracts will give you a significant edge. They are the building blocks of an autonomous, decentralized economy—and they're changing how we interact, transact, and build in the digital age.

Layla, the corporate lawyer

Layla was a corporate lawyer from London who had spent over a decade drafting contracts for multinational companies. Her days were filled with negotiations, redlines, delays, and emails flying back and forth over every clause. She lived by the motto, "Put it in writing, and make sure everyone signs." So when she heard about something called a "smart contract" from a younger intern, she laughed it off. "No code can replace a lawyer," she said with a smirk. But curiosity got the best of her.

Later that evening, Layla found herself watching a YouTube video titled *"Smart Contracts for Beginners."* What she saw made her jaw drop. It explained how agreements could be written not in legalese, but in code. These contracts lived on the blockchain, couldn't be changed, and would execute automatically once certain conditions were met. No back-and-forth. No delays. No lawyers.

Still skeptical, she dove deeper. She learned how platforms like Ethereum enabled developers to build these digital agreements using Solidity. The more she read, the more she realized these weren't "contracts" in the traditional sense—they were **autonomous programs**. Code governed the rules, execution, and resolution. You didn't need enforcement. The contract executed itself.

One example stood out. A musician uploaded a song and created a smart contract to split all revenue: 70% to him, 30% to his producer. Each time someone purchased or streamed the song using a Web3 platform, the smart contract automatically distributed the earnings. No paperwork. No accounting. No lawsuits. "That's... elegant," she whispered.

The next day, Layla called her friend Mira, a developer who had worked on blockchain projects in Dubai. "Explain smart contracts to me like I'm five," Layla said. Mira laughed and gave her a challenge: write a simple agreement where one person sends money, and another person receives a product. "Now imagine putting that logic into a blockchain program that executes without either party needing to trust each other—or a bank," Mira said.

They spent the next few evenings building a mock rental agreement. Layla defined the terms: deposit amount, rental period, and conditions for return. Mira translated them into Solidity. Once deployed on the Ethereum testnet, the contract worked exactly as written. The tenant deposited the funds, received access to a digital property, and once the lease expired, the contract automatically refunded the deposit—if no breach was recorded.

Layla was stunned. "No lawyers. No escrow. No arbitration. Just clean logic," she said. She couldn't stop thinking about how many real-world headaches this could solve: freelance contracts, royalty payments, insurance claims, real estate deals. Even marriage prenups could become programmable.

But she also saw the dangers. One wrong line of code could drain millions. Mira showed her case studies—like the 2016 DAO hack, where flawed contract logic led to one of the biggest crypto thefts in history. There were no courts to reverse it. The blockchain executed what the code said, not what the parties meant.

"Code is law," Mira said. "That's the beauty and the risk."

By the end of the month, Layla had drafted her first smart legal contract—a hybrid between traditional legal language and Solidity code. She began consulting for startups who wanted legal guidance on smart contract terms. What started as skepticism turned into a career pivot.

Layla no longer saw her job as protecting companies through words. She saw herself as a new kind of builder—helping design **digital trust** through programmable logic. She didn't just write contracts anymore. She deployed them.

And in that transformation, Layla realized something powerful: the future of law wouldn't be argued in courtrooms. It would be **executed on-chain**, one line of code at a time.

Chapter 4: Ethereum and the Rise of Decentralized Applications (dApps)

Bitcoin may have introduced the world to blockchain, but Ethereum showed us what was truly possible with it. Ethereum is the first blockchain platform that enabled **programmable smart contracts**, allowing developers to build **decentralized applications (dApps)** that operate independently of any central authority. It transformed the blockchain from a ledger into an **execution environment**—a global, trustless computer.

Ethereum was proposed by Vitalik Buterin in 2013 as a response to Bitcoin's limitations. While Bitcoin was designed purely for peer-to-peer value transfer, Ethereum was designed to be **general-purpose**. Instead of being restricted to one use case, Ethereum introduced the concept of a **Turing-complete** blockchain, capable of running any code that can be logically programmed. This allowed developers to deploy smart contracts and decentralized apps that could do anything from issuing tokens to creating entire autonomous organizations.

The Ethereum network operates on its own cryptocurrency, **Ether (ETH)**, which is used to pay for transactions and computation. Every operation on Ethereum—whether it's transferring tokens, executing a contract, or updating a data state—requires a small fee called **gas**. This ensures that developers write efficient code and that the network isn't spammed with useless computations.

The rise of Ethereum led to the explosive growth of **dApps**—applications that are open-source, decentralized, and governed by smart contracts instead of centralized servers. Examples include:

- **Uniswap** – a decentralized exchange (DEX) allowing users to swap tokens without intermediaries.
- **Aave** and **Compound** – lending protocols that allow users to earn interest or borrow crypto using collateral.
- **OpenSea** – a platform for buying and selling NFTs (non-fungible tokens).
- **DAOs** – Decentralized Autonomous Organizations that manage treasury, voting, and governance using blockchain-based rules.

What makes dApps unique is that once deployed, they cannot be changed easily. They run as written, visible to everyone on the blockchain, and not controlled by a single company. This makes them **censorship-resistant**, transparent, and accessible to anyone with an internet connection and a crypto wallet.

However, building on Ethereum also comes with challenges. Gas fees can spike during network congestion, making transactions expensive. Ethereum's original architecture was also slow, processing only about 15 transactions per second—compared to Visa's thousands. These scalability issues sparked the development of **Layer 2 solutions** like Arbitrum and Optimism, and eventually led to Ethereum's upgrade to **Proof of Stake** through Ethereum 2.0.

Another important innovation on Ethereum was the **ERC-20 token standard**, which allowed developers to create custom tokens with shared rules. This enabled the **Initial Coin Offering (ICO) boom** in 2017 and laid the foundation for the **DeFi** and **NFT** explosions years later. ERC-721 (NFTs) and ERC-1155 (multi-token assets) followed, turning Ethereum into a hub for digital creativity and decentralized finance.

In essence, Ethereum made blockchain **programmable**, unlocking a world of applications that don't rely on banks, governments, or centralized tech companies. It allowed anyone to become a creator, an investor, a lender, or a participant in decentralized systems—without gatekeepers.

Understanding Ethereum is essential if you want to go beyond investing in crypto and start **interacting with the new internet**. Whether you're minting NFTs, joining DAOs, farming DeFi yields, or building your own dApp, Ethereum is the foundation layer. It redefined what blockchain could be—and it continues to shape the future of decentralized innovation.

Luca's Ethereum story

Before Luca discovered Ethereum, his understanding of crypto was limited to Bitcoin. He thought it was just digital money—nothing more. A former game designer turned UX consultant, he was more interested in interactive tech than finance. But that changed the day he joined a Telegram group for blockchain-based game developers. That's where he heard the phrase *"dApp"—*short for **decentralized application**. Someone posted, "If Bitcoin was the calculator, Ethereum is the smartphone."

Curiosity piqued, Luca dove in. He read about how Ethereum wasn't just a digital currency—it was a **programmable blockchain**. Unlike Bitcoin, which just allowed you to send and receive money, Ethereum let you build **apps that lived on the blockchain**. These weren't hosted on AWS, nor did they have centralized control panels. They were unstoppable programs—once deployed, they just ran. Always. Everywhere.

The possibilities overwhelmed him. He imagined a game where players truly **owned their in-game assets**, traded rare swords or land directly with each other, and didn't need to ask a game publisher for permission. No central server, no banned accounts, no data deletion. Just code—and **trustless ownership**. It was exactly what he had always dreamed of building.

He spent the next few weeks learning Solidity, the programming language for Ethereum. The documentation was tough at first, but the logic was familiar. Deploy a smart contract. Store a value. Execute based on conditions. Simple in concept—powerful in effect. He deployed his first test dApp: a fantasy pet breeding game where users could buy, breed, and trade pixelated creatures. Each creature was a **non-fungible token (NFT)**—a unique asset stored on the Ethereum blockchain.

But Luca quickly hit a wall. Every time a player interacted with the game, they had to pay **gas fees**. During busy times, these fees spiked. Some users paid $40 just to mint a pet. It was unsustainable. He looked for answers and discovered **Layer 2 solutions** like Polygon and Arbitrum—networks built on top of Ethereum to reduce congestion and costs. He migrated his dApp there, and interaction fees dropped to pennies.

The more he built, the more he explored the Ethereum ecosystem. He started using **Uniswap**, a decentralized exchange where he could swap tokens without needing an account or verification. He borrowed stablecoins from **Aave**, used his crypto as collateral, and even voted in a **DAO** that governed an NFT project he liked. He wasn't just using apps—he was participating in digital economies governed by code.

What struck him most was the transparency. Every contract he interacted with could be viewed on **Etherscan**. He could read the code, verify what it did, and see every transaction ever made. There were no secrets. No black boxes. Just logic.

He began consulting for other game developers, helping them tokenize assets and move logic on-chain. He built a guild management system using smart contracts. He even created a revenue-sharing protocol for streamers using **ERC-20 tokens**. For the first time, he saw a future where developers weren't employees of platforms—they were **owners of protocols**.

Ethereum had turned him from a gamer into a builder—and from a builder into a believer. It wasn't perfect—gas fees, slow speeds, and user experience issues still existed. But it was a new frontier. One where **digital freedom and economic participation were accessible to anyone, anywhere**.

As he looked at his growing community of users—players from Brazil, Kenya, and South Korea trading game assets and earning real income—Luca realized this wasn't just tech. It was a movement.

Ethereum didn't just create a new blockchain. It created a **new internet**—one where ownership, identity, and value were controlled by the people who used it.

Chapter 5: Decentralized Finance (DeFi) — Banking Without Banks

Decentralized Finance, or **DeFi**, represents one of the most powerful use cases of blockchain technology. It's a fast-growing ecosystem of financial applications that run on decentralized networks—primarily Ethereum—allowing anyone, anywhere, to borrow, lend, earn interest, trade assets, and more, all **without traditional banks or intermediaries**. Instead of depending on trust in institutions, DeFi depends on **transparent smart contracts** and publicly verifiable code.

At its core, DeFi is about taking every function that a bank or financial institution performs—like saving, lending, insurance, investing—and rebuilding it on blockchain rails. This means financial products and services are now accessible to anyone with an internet connection and a crypto wallet. There are no credit checks, paperwork, or account managers. You interact with code, not humans. And that code **executes financial logic automatically**.

One of the earliest and most popular DeFi applications is **lending protocols**. Platforms like **Aave** and **Compound** let users deposit cryptocurrency to earn interest or use their crypto as collateral to borrow other assets. These protocols use smart contracts to automatically manage loans, interest rates, and liquidations. If your collateral drops below a certain value, the system will liquidate part of your holdings automatically. It's brutally efficient.

Another key area of DeFi is **decentralized exchanges (DEXs)** like **Uniswap** and **SushiSwap**, where users can trade tokens directly with one another. These platforms use **liquidity pools**—pools of tokens provided by users in exchange for a share of the transaction fees. Instead of using an order book like a traditional exchange, DEXs use **automated market makers (AMMs)**, which are algorithms that price assets based on supply and demand.

Then there's **yield farming** and **liquidity mining**, where users move their funds between different protocols to earn the highest return. Some even stack these strategies across platforms to maximize profits. The rewards can be high, but so can the risks—many projects are experimental, unaudited, or outright scams.

A revolutionary DeFi component is the use of **stablecoins** like **DAI**, which are pegged to the U.S. dollar but governed by decentralized protocols. These stablecoins provide price stability, making it easier to use DeFi for everyday financial activities. For example, you can earn interest on DAI, borrow against it, or use it for transactions—all without using actual dollars or touching a bank account.

One of the most innovative structures in DeFi is the **Decentralized Autonomous Organization (DAO).** These are governance systems where token holders can vote on decisions, such as interest rate changes, collateral types, or development upgrades. This creates a **community-governed financial institution** with no CEO or board of directors—just stakeholders and smart contracts.

However, DeFi isn't perfect. It's **high-risk and highly experimental**. Bugs in smart contracts have led to losses in the millions. Flash loan attacks—where hackers borrow large sums instantly and manipulate markets—have exposed vulnerabilities in many protocols. There's also the issue of **regulation**. Since DeFi operates without borders or licenses, many regulators are scrambling to figure out how to manage it.

Yet, the promise of DeFi is enormous. In regions with unstable banking systems or limited access to credit, DeFi offers a **lifeline to financial freedom**. It's also sparking innovation in financial instruments, like synthetic assets, tokenized stocks, and algorithmic insurance.

In conclusion, DeFi is a fundamental shift from centralized finance to an **open, programmable, and permissionless**

system. It's not just about disrupting banks—it's about building a **new financial internet**, where everyone can participate, innovate, and grow wealth on equal footing.

The story of Carlos MetaMask wallet

Carlos was a small business owner in Argentina. Like many in his country, he had lived through multiple financial crises—currency devaluations, frozen bank accounts, sky-high inflation. Every time he tried to save or invest, something outside of his control disrupted his plans. After losing half his savings in a bank freeze, Carlos gave up on traditional finance. He didn't trust banks, but he didn't know where else to go. That changed when a tech-savvy nephew introduced him to **DeFi**—a term that sounded like science fiction but quickly became his lifeline.

At first, Carlos didn't understand it. "How can you earn interest without a bank?" he asked. His nephew, Diego, explained how **smart contracts** and **liquidity pools** replaced bankers and spreadsheets. Carlos opened a MetaMask wallet, watched tutorials, and cautiously deposited $100 worth of DAI—a decentralized, dollar-pegged stablecoin—into a protocol called **Aave**. In a few hours, he saw a small interest accrual. "Wait... I'm actually earning without a bank?" he whispered.

He dove in deeper. He learned how lending protocols worked—how users like him could deposit stablecoins and others could borrow against their crypto. No loan officer, no paperwork, just an automatic system enforced by math. He wasn't just saving anymore—he was **earning yield**. And more importantly, no government could freeze or seize his assets.

Then Carlos discovered **Uniswap**, a decentralized exchange. Unlike traditional exchanges, it didn't rely on buyers and sellers matching orders. Instead, users like him provided tokens to **liquidity pools**, earning a share of every trade. He converted some of his ETH into different assets and experimented with providing liquidity. "It's like being the house in a casino," Diego explained. "You don't need to guess the winner—you earn from the game being played."

The most surprising moment came when Carlos stumbled onto **yield farming**. By staking tokens in certain protocols, he could earn governance tokens that represented ownership in the platform. It felt like being part of a financial co-op—only global, fast, and open 24/7. He read about **DAOs**, digital organizations governed by token holders, and even voted on a proposal to reduce interest rates in one of the platforms he used. "I've never had a vote in any bank," he said with a smile.

But it wasn't all smooth sailing. One night, chasing a 200% APY on a new DeFi project, Carlos got burned. The smart contract was unaudited. A hacker exploited it and drained the entire liquidity pool. He lost $400 overnight. The sting was sharp, but the lesson stuck. "If it sounds too good to be true, it usually is," Diego reminded him. From then on, Carlos only used protocols with strong reputations, audits, and community backing.

He also started using **stablecoins** more aggressively. Every time inflation in Argentina soared, Carlos would convert pesos into DAI to protect his savings. His friends mocked him—until their pesos lost 30% of their value in one month. Carlos didn't lose a cent. Instead, he *gained* interest.

Eventually, he started teaching others—friends, family, even local entrepreneurs—how to onboard into DeFi. He held workshops in coffee shops, showed farmers how to earn interest on savings, and helped freelancers get paid in crypto and avoid banking delays. He had become a **bridge between two worlds**: the old system that failed him and the new one that empowered him.

For Carlos, DeFi wasn't just an investment strategy. It was **financial independence**, built not on institutions, but on code. No teller windows. No frozen accounts. Just transparency, autonomy, and opportunity—for anyone bold enough to take control of their own money.

Chapter 6: NFTs — Digital Ownership in the Blockchain Era

NFTs, or **non-fungible tokens**, are one of the most high-profile applications of blockchain technology—and one of the most misunderstood. While they first made headlines through digital art sales and meme culture, their significance reaches far beyond collectibles. NFTs represent a new way to **verify, own, and transfer digital assets** in a decentralized, transparent, and secure manner. In simple terms, NFTs make digital property **provable and portable**.

Let's break it down. The term "non-fungible" means that the item is **unique and not interchangeable**. This is different from something like Bitcoin or dollars, where each unit is identical and can be swapped freely. With NFTs, each token is distinct—just like physical items such as real estate, art, or concert tickets. This uniqueness is what gives NFTs their value.

NFTs are typically built on Ethereum using standards like **ERC-721** or **ERC-1155**. These tokens are managed by **smart contracts** that assign metadata, ownership, and transferability. The blockchain keeps a **permanent record of ownership**, so it's easy to track the original creator, the current owner, and every transaction in between. This concept is often referred to as **"digital provenance."**

One of the most visible use cases of NFTs is in **digital art**. Artists can mint their creations as NFTs and sell them directly to buyers on platforms like **OpenSea**, **Rarible**, or **Foundation**. When a piece is sold, the creator can even program the NFT to **automatically earn royalties** every time the artwork is resold. This gives artists ongoing income and unprecedented control over their work.

But NFTs go beyond art. They are being used for:

- **Music rights** and royalties
- **Virtual land** and real estate in metaverses (like Decentraland or The Sandbox)
- **Event tickets** that are tamper-proof and resellable
- **Gaming assets** like weapons, characters, or skins
- **Digital identity**, diplomas, and certificates
- **Tokenized physical assets**, like luxury watches or rare wines

NFTs are also central to the emerging world of **Web3**—where users own their data, digital goods, and online identities. In this context, your NFT might represent your username, avatar, or credentials that you carry across platforms.

There are challenges, of course. One is the **environmental impact** of minting NFTs on Proof of Work blockchains (although Ethereum's shift to Proof of Stake has helped reduce this). Another is **speculation and scams**—many NFT collections are created with little substance, and buyers are lured by hype rather than utility. There are also concerns around **intellectual property**, since NFTs represent ownership of a token, not necessarily the copyright of the asset it points to.

Despite these issues, the potential is massive. NFTs turn the internet into a place where **ownership is built-in**. They give creators and communities tools to build **digital economies**—where fans, artists, and collectors can collaborate and share value directly, without middlemen.

In the future, we may see NFTs powering everything from medical records to real estate deeds to immersive metaverse experiences. Whether as art, access keys, or identity layers, NFTs are laying the groundwork for a more **interactive and owner-driven digital world**.

Maya's story

Maya was a digital illustrator from Manila who had been creating art since she could hold a pencil. She had a modest following on Instagram and a small Etsy shop where she sold prints of her work. But even with a loyal fanbase, making a living was a constant struggle. She had to manage inventory, deal with shipping, and navigate platforms that took huge commissions. Worst of all, she saw her work reposted and stolen online almost daily, with no way to prove it was hers.

Everything changed the day her friend Nico told her about **NFTs**. "You can mint your art on the blockchain and sell it as a digital original," he said. "People are making thousands without even printing anything." At first, Maya thought it was just another tech bubble. But curiosity got the better of her.

She watched tutorials on how to mint NFTs using platforms like **OpenSea** and **Rarible**, set up a MetaMask wallet, and learned how to list her work using **Ethereum-based smart contracts**. Her first piece was a moody digital painting of a lunar goddess. She minted it, added a description, and listed it for 0.1 ETH. She had no expectations.

It sold within 48 hours.

The buyer sent her a message: "Thank you. I love this piece. I'll display it in my metaverse gallery." Maya was stunned. For the first time, someone didn't just download her art—they **owned it**, verified on the blockchain. And she could prove she was the creator, forever.

What excited her more was the **royalty feature**. She added a 10% royalty to her NFTs, meaning every time her artwork resold, she would automatically receive a cut. This wasn't just one-time income. It was a **passive revenue stream**, programmed into the contract itself.

Maya began minting more. She experimented with animations, collaborations, and even audio-reactive visuals. Soon, collectors were bidding on her drops. She joined Twitter Spaces with other artists, entered NFT exhibitions, and connected with a global community that supported her creativity in a way no gallery ever had.

But it wasn't all glamor. During the NFT market boom, Maya received dozens of spam offers. She accidentally minted a piece on the wrong blockchain once and lost money on gas fees. And during one low point, an imposter minted her early work and tried to sell it. Thankfully, she had the originals on-chain with timestamps—proof that the impostor was a fraud. "Blockchain doesn't lie," Nico reminded her.

As the hype cooled, Maya shifted focus to **utility-based NFTs**. She launched a collection that doubled as access passes to monthly digital workshops. Another series granted holders discounts on commissions. Some of her NFTs even unlocked behind-the-scenes videos of her creative process. She wasn't just selling art anymore—she was building a **digital ecosystem** around her creativity.

She also explored **gaming NFTs**, collaborating with developers to design characters and environments that players could own and trade. Her work began appearing in metaverse galleries, online games, and even on digital billboards during virtual fashion weeks. The line between art and utility blurred—and Maya thrived in that space.

NFTs gave Maya more than money. They gave her **freedom and validation**. No longer dependent on platforms or middlemen, she became her own brand, her own gallery, her own marketplace. Her collectors weren't just buyers—they were supporters, stakeholders, and members of a growing community.

One night, as she watched her NFT dashboard light up with a new resale notification, Maya smiled. What had once felt like a chaotic internet of theft and anonymity had become a place where **ownership mattered**, where creators had power, and where art could truly live, breathe, and evolve—on the blockchain.

Chapter 7: Blockchain Use Cases Beyond Crypto

While blockchain is often associated with cryptocurrency, its applications extend far beyond Bitcoin or even Ethereum. In fact, blockchain's most revolutionary impact may be in industries where **trust, transparency, verification, and efficiency** are critical—but where central systems are inefficient, corrupt, or fragile. The truth is, blockchain is not just a financial innovation—it's an **infrastructure revolution**.

1. Supply Chain Management

One of the earliest and most promising uses of blockchain is in **supply chain tracking**. Traditionally, supply chains involve multiple parties—manufacturers, shippers, customs agents, retailers—and trust is maintained by paperwork and institutional relationships. This system is prone to fraud, loss, and inefficiency.

Blockchain changes that by offering **real-time, tamper-proof tracking** of goods. Companies like IBM and Walmart use blockchain to monitor food origins, ensuring freshness and safety. For example, if there's an outbreak of E.

coli, blockchain can pinpoint which batch of lettuce is affected within seconds—rather than days.

2. Healthcare and Medical Records

In healthcare, patient records are often fragmented and hard to access. A blockchain-based health record system can offer **secure, interoperable, and patient-controlled access** to data. Patients can control who sees their medical history and share records across borders or between providers without the fear of data leaks or tampering.

Some startups and even national health systems are experimenting with **blockchain-powered vaccination records**, genetic data storage, and prescription tracking—promising better outcomes, fewer errors, and more ethical use of data.

3. Real Estate and Land Ownership

Real estate is bogged down by **bureaucracy, fraud, and manual processes**. Deeds can be forged, lost, or duplicated. In some developing countries, land ownership records are either nonexistent or easily manipulated. Blockchain offers a secure, transparent, and permanent ledger for property rights.

Smart contracts can automate title transfers, and once recorded on-chain, ownership is verifiable and immutable.

Governments in places like Georgia and Sweden are testing blockchain-based land registries to reduce fraud and improve efficiency.

4. Digital Identity and Authentication

In an increasingly online world, **digital identity** is crucial—but also vulnerable. Most users rely on centralized systems (Google, Facebook, government IDs) to prove who they are. This creates honeypots for hackers and surveillance risks.

Blockchain allows for **self-sovereign identity**, where users control their own credentials using encrypted, decentralized identifiers. Whether it's logging into services, accessing age-restricted content, or applying for a loan, identity can be verified cryptographically—without giving up privacy.

5. Voting and Governance

Elections are foundational to democracy, yet election fraud, low turnout, and lack of transparency are common issues worldwide. Blockchain-based voting systems can offer **verifiable, tamper-proof, and auditable elections**, where every vote is counted and time-stamped, and voters can confirm their own submission—without revealing their identity.

Several pilot programs have explored blockchain voting in shareholder meetings, local elections, and organizational governance. While not without challenges (like accessibility and privacy), it shows strong potential.

6. Education and Credentials

Academic degrees and certifications are easily forged. With blockchain, institutions can issue **verifiable diplomas** that live permanently on a public ledger. Employers or universities can instantly verify authenticity. Students can also build a blockchain-based portfolio of achievements, licenses, and learning progress.

7. Energy and Sustainability

Blockchain is powering **peer-to-peer energy trading**, where homeowners with solar panels sell excess energy to neighbors without going through utility companies. It's also being used to track carbon credits, verify sustainable sourcing, and reward eco-friendly behavior with tokens.

Blockchain's value lies in **trust through decentralization**. Wherever there's a need to prove ownership, record transactions, enforce agreements, or eliminate middlemen, blockchain offers a more secure and efficient solution. As you look beyond crypto investments, remember: **the technology powering them is already reshaping the world.**

How Amara learned about supply chain innovation.

Amara was a logistics manager for a large agricultural export company in Kenya. Every day, she oversaw the movement of coffee beans, avocados, and macadamia nuts from rural farms to international buyers. But the supply chain was a mess. Documents were misplaced. Trucks arrived late. And verifying that a shipment actually came from a certified organic farm? Nearly impossible. Corruption and delays were routine. Frustrated, Amara searched for a better system—and stumbled upon blockchain.

She first heard about it in a webinar on **supply chain innovation**. A speaker described how blockchain could record each step of a product's journey—from farm to warehouse to port to shelf—on a transparent, tamper-proof ledger. It wasn't just about trust—it was about **traceability**. Every actor in the chain could upload data, photos, or certifications, and the final buyer could verify everything without relying on emails or printed receipts.

Inspired, Amara pitched a pilot project to her company. She partnered with a blockchain startup and worked with local farmers to tag each batch of goods with a **QR code linked to**

a blockchain ledger. As the produce moved through the supply chain, workers scanned the code at each checkpoint. Amara watched in awe as a coffee shipment updated live across every node. Her team in Nairobi saw the same data as the European buyer. There was no room for excuses. No hiding. Just data-backed truth.

At the same time, Amara's sister, Leila—a nurse at a private clinic—was exploring blockchain in **healthcare**. Patients frequently struggled to get their full medical history when transferring between hospitals. Leila joined a trial where patients controlled their **blockchain-based health profiles**, granting temporary access to doctors with a cryptographic key. It reduced duplicate testing, misdiagnoses, and improved outcomes. The difference was night and day.

Amara was blown away. "This technology isn't just for crypto bros," she laughed. "It's infrastructure for everything."

Later that year, she read about countries using blockchain for **land titles**. A friend of hers in Lagos had nearly lost her inherited property because local officials tried to forge documents. On a blockchain registry, that could never happen. Ownership was **immutable**, timestamped, and publicly verifiable. She imagined how much injustice could be prevented if land deeds in Africa were on-chain.

As elections approached in Kenya, the topic of **voting integrity** dominated the news. Amara wondered if blockchain could help there, too. A prototype system had been piloted in Estonia, where voters used their smartphones to cast encrypted, blockchain-verified ballots. Every vote was traceable, and citizens could independently verify that their vote was counted. She shared the idea on social media—and was surprised by how many others resonated with it.

Amara's journey led her to speak at international conferences, where she presented her supply chain success. She was no longer just a manager—she was a pioneer. She collaborated with universities exploring **educational credentialing** on blockchain, where diplomas were issued as verifiable NFTs, eliminating fake degrees. She even bought solar panels and joined a **peer-to-peer energy grid**, selling excess power to neighbors and tracking it all on-chain.

For Amara, blockchain was no longer abstract. It was a **real-world operating system**—one that could eliminate paperwork, corruption, inefficiency, and exclusion. And it wasn't controlled by any one company or country. It was **global, neutral, and fair**.

As she walked through the warehouse one afternoon, watching a scanner update a shipment record on the blockchain, Amara smiled. "It's not about Bitcoin anymore," she said. "It's about building a world where truth lives in the code."

Chapter 8: Risks, Scams, and Security in the Blockchain World

As revolutionary as blockchain technology is, the space is still young, volatile, and filled with risks. For all its transparency and decentralization, blockchain is not immune to human error, bad actors, and technical vulnerabilities. To navigate this ecosystem safely, users must understand the **common risks, common scams, and core security practices** that protect digital assets.

1. Phishing and Social Engineering

Just like in traditional finance, many crypto-related scams begin with phishing. This is when scammers trick users into revealing private information, such as seed phrases or private keys, by impersonating trustworthy platforms or support agents. Fake websites and fake social media profiles are rampant. A single slip—entering your seed phrase on a fake MetaMask site—can drain your wallet within seconds.

The solution is simple but strict: **Never share your private keys or seed phrase**. Always double-check URLs, bookmark trusted sites, and verify official sources. Use browser security tools, and be skeptical of any message asking for your wallet info.

2. Rug Pulls and Scam Projects

In decentralized finance and NFT spaces, a "rug pull" refers to a project that looks legitimate but is designed to **take investor money and disappear**. This often happens with new tokens or NFT collections. Developers promote a token, pump the price, and then drain the liquidity or abandon the roadmap, leaving investors with worthless assets.

Before investing in any new project:

- Research the team (are they doxxed and reputable?)
- Check if the smart contract is **audited** by a trusted security firm.
- Look at token distribution—if a small number of wallets hold the majority of supply, it's a red flag.
- Avoid hype-only projects with no utility or working product.

3. Smart Contract Exploits

Smart contracts are code—and like any code, they can contain bugs. When deployed on a blockchain, a flawed contract can be exploited by hackers, often resulting in **millions in stolen**

funds. Because blockchains are immutable, mistakes usually cannot be undone.

Major DeFi hacks have occurred due to:

- Flash loan attacks (temporarily manipulating prices for profit)
- Re-entrancy bugs (contracts calling themselves recursively)
- Poor access controls and overexposed admin rights

Mitigation comes through **audits, code reviews, and bug bounties**. If you're using a DeFi protocol, choose platforms with a security-first reputation and public track records.

4. Private Key and Wallet Risks

Your wallet—like MetaMask or Trust Wallet—is your gateway to the blockchain. But losing access to it means losing everything. If you lose your private key or recovery phrase, there's **no password reset option**. Similarly, if malware infects your device or a screen recorder captures your inputs, your funds can be stolen without any hope of recovery.

To stay safe:

- Use **hardware wallets** (like Ledger or Trezor) for storing large balances.
- Write down your recovery phrase and store it **offline**, preferably in multiple safe locations.
- Enable 2FA and use secure devices.
- Avoid using browser wallets on shared or public computers.

5. Regulatory and Legal Risks

Blockchain operates across borders, but regulation is still catching up. Depending on where you live, participating in crypto may expose you to tax liabilities, reporting requirements, or even restrictions. Governments may ban certain tokens, exchanges, or wallet types without notice.

It's crucial to:

- Stay updated with crypto regulation in your jurisdiction.
- Track and report your **crypto income and capital gains** properly.
- Use regulated on-ramps and consider working with a crypto-savvy accountant.

6. Psychological and Emotional Traps

The crypto market is highly volatile. Scams often prey on **FOMO (fear of missing out)** or unrealistic profit expectations. Many users make poor decisions based on hype, greed, or panic. Day trading, impulse buying, and "apeing into" tokens without research are common pitfalls.

Practice **emotional discipline**:

- Set goals and stick to a strategy.
- Only invest what you can afford to lose.
- Diversify your portfolio.
- Don't chase trends blindly.

Blockchain offers financial freedom—but with it comes **full responsibility**. There's no customer service line in crypto. You are your own bank, your own security guard, and your own investigator. By staying educated, alert, and skeptical, you can protect your assets and thrive in the decentralized world.

How Ethan's funds disappeared

Ethan considered himself tech-savvy. A web developer from Toronto, he had dabbled in crypto since 2017, built a few smart contract experiments on testnets, and had grown his ETH holdings slowly over the years. But in early 2021, during the height of the NFT and DeFi boom, he let his guard down—and it nearly cost him everything.

It started with a message on Discord. A moderator from a DAO he had recently joined reached out privately, claiming there was a limited staking opportunity to earn governance tokens. The message was convincing—there were links, branding, and even screenshots of other members earning rewards. Without hesitation, Ethan clicked the link, connected his wallet, and approved the transaction.

Within seconds, all of his funds vanished.

Panic set in. He scoured the blockchain explorer, watching his ETH move across wallets and vanish into a mixer. The "moderator" had been a scammer, and Ethan had fallen for a **phishing attack**—a social engineering trick that preyed on his trust and urgency. He hadn't been hacked. He had unknowingly given them permission.

The worst part? There was no undo button. No customer support. No reversing the transaction. In the blockchain world, **you are your own bank—and your own last line of defense**.

Determined not to make the same mistake twice, Ethan went into full research mode. He read about **rug pulls**—those sudden disappearances of "promising" crypto projects. He remembered watching a token moon one week and crash to zero the next. Digging into the contracts, he found out the developers had retained over 80% of the supply and dumped it on retail buyers. "It wasn't just volatility," he realized. "It was planned."

He also learned how **smart contract exploits** worked. One night, he read a case study on a DeFi protocol that was drained through a re-entrancy bug—a subtle coding flaw that allowed a hacker to drain liquidity before the contract updated its balance. He stared at the line of code that caused it all. One function call in the wrong place had led to a $30 million loss. "Code is law," he thought, "but bugs are still bugs."

Ethan began storing his assets more carefully. He bought a **hardware wallet** and moved his long-term holdings offline. He wrote down his recovery phrase—twice—and stored each copy in different safe places. He started using **burner wallets** for testing new dApps and never connected his main wallet to unknown protocols.

He also adjusted his mindset. Gone were the days of FOMO-fueled trades. He stopped aping into meme coins and started vetting projects properly. He checked audit reports, read whitepapers with skepticism, and tracked token distribution. If a project didn't have a public team or a working product, he passed.

Over time, he became a resource for others. He wrote blog posts about crypto safety, hosted workshops on Discord, and even consulted startups on secure wallet design. He no longer saw crypto security as optional—it was foundational. "You wouldn't leave your physical wallet on the street," he told others. "So don't do it digitally."

But perhaps the most important change was psychological. Ethan accepted that **risk was part of the game**. Even the best protocols could be attacked. Even the most careful users could make mistakes. But what mattered was education, process, and the ability to learn quickly.

He wasn't trying to eliminate risk. He was learning to manage it.

And in the decentralized world—where responsibility couldn't be outsourced—**that made all the difference**.

Chapter 9: The Future of Blockchain — Web3, Metaverse & Global Disruption

Blockchain is no longer just a financial technology—it's becoming the **foundation of a new digital era**. As the internet evolves beyond static websites and centralized platforms, we are entering the age of **Web3**—a decentralized internet powered by blockchain, cryptocurrencies, smart contracts, and token economies. This transition promises to reshape how we **communicate, create, collaborate, and earn** in the digital world.

1. Web3 — A Decentralized Internet

Web1 was read-only. Web2 became interactive—bringing social media, cloud computing, and user-generated content—but it was still controlled by centralized platforms like Google, Meta, and Amazon. Web3 introduces a **user-owned internet**, where control, identity, and value flow directly to individuals and communities, not corporations.

In Web3, users own digital assets (like NFTs), access services through wallets (not usernames), and govern platforms through tokens and DAOs. Apps are **decentralized**, often running on blockchains or peer-to-peer networks.

Monetization is direct and programmable, thanks to smart contracts. This rebalances power in favor of the user.

2. The Metaverse — Digital Life on Blockchain

The **metaverse** refers to immersive, persistent digital worlds where people interact, play, work, trade, and socialize. Think of it as the 3D evolution of the internet. Blockchain provides the infrastructure to **verify digital ownership, identity, and scarcity** inside these virtual spaces.

In blockchain-based metaverses like **Decentraland**, **The Sandbox**, and **Otherside**, users can:

- Buy and sell **virtual real estate**
- Display and trade **NFTs**
- Attend concerts, meetings, or social events
- Build games, shops, and experiences
- Earn income through play-to-earn mechanics

Each asset—whether land, a wearable, or an avatar—can be tokenized as an NFT, ensuring true digital ownership. This opens new economies where creators, developers, artists, and gamers can earn without middlemen.

3. DAOs and Decentralized Governance

DAOs (Decentralized Autonomous Organizations) represent the governance layer of Web3. They allow communities to **coordinate and make decisions democratically**, using tokens as votes. From funding startups to managing DeFi protocols to running metaverse cities, DAOs are redefining leadership and organizational design.

This model enables **borderless collaboration**—people from all over the world pooling resources and skills, governed by transparent rules encoded on-chain. DAOs may one day rival corporations in scope, efficiency, and impact.

4. Tokenization of Everything

Blockchain allows for the **tokenization of real-world assets**—including stocks, real estate, carbon credits, and intellectual property. This creates more liquidity, fractional ownership, and access for investors around the world. For example:

- A building can be split into 10,000 tokens, allowing small investors to co-own it.
- Music royalties can be tokenized and sold directly to fans.

- Luxury items, art, and even wine collections are now represented by NFTs and traded globally.

This democratizes access to investment opportunities and enables **micro-economies** previously impossible in traditional finance.

5. Global Economic Impact and Disruption

Blockchain is likely to disrupt entire industries:

- **Finance**: DeFi already challenges banking models.
- **Gaming**: Play-to-earn and on-chain economies reward time and participation.
- **Social Media**: Users control their data, monetize directly, and avoid censorship.
- **Education**: Credentialing and learning paths are verifiable and portable.
- **Healthcare**: Decentralized data sharing improves access and security.

In emerging markets, blockchain could **bank the unbanked**, reduce corruption, and create global earning opportunities via digital work, DeFi, or DAOs. It levels the playing field.

6. Challenges Ahead

The future of blockchain is bright—but not guaranteed. Key challenges include:

- **Scalability**: Can blockchain handle billions of users?
- **Interoperability**: Can chains talk to each other effectively?
- **Regulation**: How will governments adapt or resist?
- **Education**: Will the average person understand how to participate safely?
- **Energy Efficiency**: Proof of Stake and Layer 2s help, but it remains a concern.

In conclusion, blockchain is not just a passing trend—it's a **core pillar of the future internet and global economy**. From identity to governance to entertainment, blockchain is building a world where trust is programmable, ownership is digital, and opportunity is decentralized. Understanding this now means leading, not lagging, in the next era of human progress.

Jules story

Jules had always been a futurist at heart. As a UI/UX designer from Amsterdam, she had worked on dozens of sleek websites and mobile apps—but lately, it all felt repetitive. Centralized platforms, data-hungry corporations, and locked-in user experiences made her feel like the internet had stopped evolving. Then she stumbled upon a hackathon titled "Build the Future: Web3 & Metaverse" and decided to participate out of curiosity. What she found there changed everything.

On the first day, she was introduced to **Web3**—a vision of the internet where users owned their data, controlled their identity, and earned directly from their participation. Instead of building platforms that extracted value, developers were creating systems that **shared value**. Wallets replaced logins, smart contracts replaced backend logic, and tokens represented access, ownership, or influence.

Jules joined a team building a decentralized social media platform. Unlike Instagram or Twitter, there was no central server. Posts were stored on IPFS, identities were linked to blockchain wallets, and content creators earned tokens based on community engagement. The kicker? The users themselves voted on platform upgrades through a **DAO**. "This is what the internet should have been from the start," she thought.

But what really blew her mind was the **metaverse**. During the hackathon, she stepped into a VR space on **The Sandbox** where avatars danced, collaborated, and built digital stores. She purchased a virtual plot of land using ETH, designed a showroom to display her 3D art, and minted wearable NFTs users could buy. She wasn't just designing interfaces anymore—she was **designing experiences in a new dimension**.

Her metaverse gallery quickly attracted attention. One visitor asked if they could host a live poetry reading there. Another wanted to rent it out for a fashion show. "Real estate... in the metaverse," she laughed to herself. But the payments were real, the interactions were real, and the ownership was **verifiable on-chain**.

Through these projects, Jules met developers working on **tokenizing real-world assets**—fractionalizing buildings, music royalties, and art into tradeable NFTs. She joined a DAO investing in renewable energy credits and began consulting for a startup that issued **blockchain-based university diplomas**. Suddenly, every system she thought was static—education, property, finance, work—was being **reimagined from the ground up**.

But it wasn't all utopian. She saw firsthand the challenges: slow blockchains, expensive gas fees, UX hurdles, and legal ambiguity. Some users lost funds through user error. Others were locked out due to lost keys. The space was still raw. Still being built. Still uncertain.

Yet Jules stayed. Not because it was easy—but because it felt important. She saw **creators monetizing without middlemen**, gamers owning their progress, teachers building decentralized course libraries, and musicians running their own economies. She saw a world **less dependent on big platforms** and more empowering to individuals.

Her proudest moment came six months later when she launched her own project—**Aether City**—a community-owned digital district that hosted art, education, and open markets inside the metaverse. Every decision was voted on by holders of $AETHER, the governance token. And every asset—from benches to buildings—was co-created by artists around the world.

As she stood on her digital rooftop, watching avatars arrive for a community meeting, Jules smiled. "This isn't just tech," she said aloud. "It's a movement."

And in that moment, surrounded by code, creativity, and community, she realized the future of blockchain wasn't about crypto charts or coins.

It was about **freedom, ownership, and reimagining the world together.**

Chapter 10: How to Get Started With Blockchain — Wallets, Exchanges, and Earning Crypto

Now that you understand how blockchain works and the incredible range of applications it powers, the next step is learning how to **get started safely and confidently**. Whether your goal is to invest, build, earn, or just explore, you'll need to understand the basic tools and processes involved in entering the blockchain ecosystem. This chapter will walk you through the essentials: setting up a wallet, choosing an exchange, buying crypto, securing your assets, and beginning to earn in the decentralized economy.

1. Crypto Wallets — Your Digital Keys to the Blockchain

A **crypto wallet** is a software or hardware tool that allows you to interact with blockchain networks. It stores your **private keys**, which are required to access and control your assets. Think of it as your digital identity and vault.

There are two main types:

- **Hot wallets**: Software wallets like **MetaMask**, **Trust Wallet**, or **Coinbase Wallet** that connect to the internet. They are great for day-to-day use and DeFi interactions.

- **Cold wallets**: **Hardware wallets** like **Ledger** or **Trezor**, which store your keys offline. Ideal for long-term storage and high-value portfolios.

When you create a wallet, you'll receive a **12- or 24-word seed phrase**—your master key. Write this down and store it safely offline. Never share it. If someone has it, they can access your funds. If you lose it, there's no way to recover your wallet.

2. Exchanges — Where You Buy and Sell Crypto

To buy your first crypto, you'll typically use a **centralized exchange (CEX)** such as:

- **Coinbase** (USA)
- **Binance** (Global)
- **Kraken**
- **Crypto.com**

These platforms allow you to deposit fiat (like USD, EUR) and purchase cryptocurrencies. They are beginner-friendly, offer mobile apps, and include ID verification (KYC). Once you've bought crypto, you can **withdraw it to your personal wallet** for full control.

Alternatively, **decentralized exchanges (DEXs)** like **Uniswap** or **PancakeSwap** let you trade directly from your wallet—no registration needed. But you must already own crypto to use them.

3. How to Buy Crypto (Step-by-Step)

1. Create an account on a CEX (like Coinbase).
2. Verify your identity (upload ID).
3. Add a payment method (bank transfer or card).
4. Buy crypto (e.g., Bitcoin, Ethereum).
5. Transfer to your private wallet for security.

Start with small amounts and familiarize yourself with transfer times and fees. Practice sending crypto from the exchange to your wallet to understand how addresses and gas fees work.

4. How to Earn Crypto (Passive & Active)

Once you've secured your wallet and understand how to transact, you can begin to **earn crypto**:

- **Staking**: Lock your tokens in a protocol to help secure the network and earn rewards (e.g., ETH, ADA, SOL).
- **Yield Farming**: Provide liquidity on DeFi platforms

like Aave, Compound, or Yearn and earn interest.

- **Play-to-Earn (P2E)**: Play blockchain-based games that reward you in tokens or NFTs.
- **Learn-to-Earn**: Platforms like Coinbase Earn and RabbitHole pay you to complete crypto education tasks.
- **Freelance and Work**: Accept crypto payments for digital services using platforms like BitWage or Request Network.
- **Run a Node**: Technical users can run validator or storage nodes and earn income (e.g., Helium, Filecoin).

5. Best Practices for Beginners

- **Double-check wallet addresses** before sending funds.
- **Use two-factor authentication (2FA)** on all exchange accounts.
- **Avoid storing large amounts in exchanges**—not your keys, not your crypto.
- **Never click unknown links or approve unknown wallet transactions**.

- **Track your activity and taxes** using tools like CoinTracker or Koinly.

The key to success in blockchain is **curiosity, security, and consistency**. Start small, learn by doing, and gradually expand your knowledge. The sooner you begin experimenting with wallets, exchanges, and on-chain tools, the faster you'll unlock opportunities in this new financial frontier.

Now, let's talk about Nina.

Nina had watched the crypto world from the sidelines for years. A freelance writer in Berlin, she'd seen friends talk about NFTs, DeFi, and metaverse projects—but every time she looked into it, the jargon felt overwhelming. Seed phrases? Gas fees? Hot wallets? It all sounded more like spy tech than personal finance. But after writing a research piece on blockchain education, Nina realized something: **you don't have to be a developer to participate—you just need to start**.

So she set a goal: buy her first cryptocurrency, store it in her own wallet, and experiment with earning. No more passive reading. It was time to act.

Her first step was setting up a **MetaMask wallet**. She installed the browser extension, followed the prompts, and carefully wrote down her 12-word recovery phrase in a notebook—not on her computer. Every tutorial said the same thing: **"If you lose this, you lose access forever."** She felt a bit of pressure, but also a sense of empowerment. This was her key. No bank. No password reset. Just her and the blockchain.

Next, she created an account on **Coinbase**, a well-known crypto exchange with a clean interface. After verifying her identity, she linked her debit card and purchased $100 worth of ETH. Within minutes, it showed up in her exchange wallet. She felt a thrill—she finally owned cryptocurrency. But the real shift happened when she **withdrew the ETH to her MetaMask**.

Watching the transaction confirm on **Etherscan**, she realized she was participating in a global network, not a walled-off app. Her ETH didn't live in a bank or server—it lived **on the blockchain**, and only she could access it.

With ETH in her wallet, Nina began exploring. She visited **Uniswap**, a decentralized exchange, and swapped a small portion of her ETH for a governance token. It was her first DEX transaction. She paid attention to the gas fee, checked the slippage, and confirmed the swap. The token appeared in her wallet moments later. “That was smoother than I expected,” she thought.

Curious about earning, she explored **staking**. She didn’t want to run a validator node, but learned she could stake ETH through platforms like **Lido** or **Rocket Pool** and earn passive rewards. With just a few clicks, she staked a portion of her holdings and watched her balance slowly grow.

She also tested **Coinbase Earn**, where watching short videos and answering quizzes rewarded her with tokens. It felt like learning and earning at the same time. She read about freelancers accepting crypto and even added her wallet address to her portfolio website.

Along the way, she made mistakes. She accidentally sent a token to the wrong network once. Another time, she forgot to leave enough ETH for gas and couldn’t complete a transaction until she added more. But each misstep taught her more than any article ever could.

What surprised Nina most was how **freeing** it felt. No one asked her for permission. No one took a cut. No one could freeze her funds or deny her access. Her digital wallet, once intimidating, now felt like a **passport to the future**.

She started journaling her crypto journey, eventually turning it into a blog. Readers reached out, asking how to get started. She helped friends set up wallets, guided artists through minting NFTs, and explained gas fees in plain English. In less than six months, she went from a hesitant observer to a confident guide.

Nina's takeaway was simple: **blockchain doesn't reward perfection—it rewards participation**. And the sooner you take that first step, the sooner you stop being a spectator and start becoming a builder in a new world.

Epilogue: The Invisible Revolution

As we close this chapter on the blockchain, it's important to pause and reflect—not just on the technical details or investment strategies, but on the broader transformation that's quietly unfolding around us. What began as a fringe idea in a whitepaper in 2008 has grown into a global movement reshaping how we define **trust, value, identity, and power** in the digital world.

Blockchain is not just another wave of technology. It's a **paradigm shift**. It challenges the status quo that has long favored centralized control, opaque systems, and gatekeepers. It empowers individuals to become their own banks, creators, and decision-makers—without asking for permission. In many ways, blockchain is not about technology at all—it's about **freedom, transparency, and decentralization**.

If you've made it through this book, you've already crossed a threshold that most never reach. You now understand the foundational pieces—what a blockchain is, how it works, and why it matters. You've explored smart contracts, NFTs, DeFi, and the metaverse. You've seen the risks, the scams, and the precautions. You've met characters and creators building the future one block at a time. And most importantly, you've been given a roadmap to begin.

But this journey is just beginning.

In the coming years, blockchain will quietly integrate into your life—even if you don't realize it. Your passport might be a verifiable credential stored in your digital wallet. Your paycheck might arrive in a stablecoin. Your favorite artist might drop exclusive content as NFTs. You might vote in a DAO. And your child's first job might take place entirely in a virtual world, governed by smart contracts and incentivized by tokens.

The shift is already underway in every sector—**finance, healthcare, law, gaming, education, supply chain, and identity**. Blockchain won't replace everything, but it will touch almost everything. Not because it's trendy—but because it's more **efficient, secure, and fair**.

Still, this power comes with responsibility. Blockchain puts you in control—but also makes you accountable. There's no reset button, no help desk, no central authority to undo mistakes. That's the price of sovereignty. But it's also the beauty of it. For the first time in digital history, your assets, your identity, and your future are truly yours.

So where do you go from here?

- Start using a wallet regularly.

- Try sending and receiving crypto.
- Explore a DAO or a DeFi app.
- Mint an NFT or collect one.
- Read whitepapers. Join communities. Stay curious.

You don't have to do everything. Just **do something**. Every action—no matter how small—helps you learn, adapt, and unlock the potential of this new world.

The blockchain revolution isn't loud. It's happening quietly—line by line, block by block, wallet by wallet. But its impact will be felt for generations.

And now, you're a part of it.

Welcome to the decentralized future.

www.ingramcontent.com/pod-product-compliance
Lightning Source LLC
LaVergne TN
LVHW022021200926
848481LV00007B/2481
* 9 7 9 8 3 4 9 6 4 2 7 8 4 *